MEN-AT-ARMS SERIES

EDITOR: MARTIN WINDROW
ALBAN BOOK SERVICES

The Royal Green Jackets

Text by CHRISTOPHER WILKINSON-LATHAM
Colour plates by MICHAEL ROFFE

OSPREY PUBLISHING LIMITED

Published in 1975 by
Osprey Publishing Ltd, 12–14 Long Acre,
London WC2E 9LP
Member Company of the George Philip Group

ISBN 0 85045 249 X

Printed in Great Britain
Monochrome by BAS Printers Limited,
Wallop, Hampshire
Colour by Barnicotts Ltd, Taunton, Somerset

Early History of Component Regiments

43rd Regiment

Originally raised as the 54th Regiment of Foot by Colonel Fowke, under a Letter of Service dated 3 January 1741, they served on the island of Minorca during the latter stages of the War of the Austrian Succession, returning home in 1747. Following the usual reductions in the army by the disbandment of regiments in times of peace, the 54th were renumbered the 43rd Regiment of Foot.

It was not until 1759, during the fighting in North America, that the 43rd gained its first battle honour at Quebec where, in a brilliant example of combined operations, General Wolfe's small force disembarked about a mile west of the town and on the night of 12–13 September made a surprise landing, scaled the Heights of Abraham and by dawn were positioned on the Plain. The outcome of the battle and the whole future of Canada was more or less decided by one devastating volley from the British which broke the French line. The 43rd were in the centre of the British line and were not as heavily engaged as the flanks. Quebec finally surrendered on the 17 September.

During the winter of 1759, the British were occupied in holding the ground they'd won, defending the town against the French attempts to retake it. Before returning to England in July 1764, the regiment was engaged in the capture of Martinique and Havana and garrison duty on the island of Jamaica.

The year 1775, saw the 43rd once more on active service on the North American continent, where the colonists were in open rebellion. During the American War of Independence the regiment saw much hard and varied service, which included the battle of Bunker Hill where, for the first time, they fought alongside the 52nd Regiment. They served through the rest of the war under Howe, Clinton and Cornwallis until the surrender of the British at Yorktown.

After spending a year as prisoners of war, the 43rd returned to England and found that, under a Royal Warrant of 31 August, 1782, they had been conferred with a County title in addition to

Private, 43rd Regiment, c. 1741 (**National Army Museum**)

3

their number, that of 'Monmouthshire'.

In 1794, the 43rd arrived at Barbados in time to take part in the attack on Martinique. They then moved on to St. Lucia and finally at Guadaloupe, where they remained in occupation until, outnumbered, decimated by disease and without reinforcements, they were forced to capitulate to the French. After an exchange of prisoners the skeleton of the regiment returned to England from where, after having augmented their numbers and re-equipped, they returned to the West Indies in 1797. Of the 1,000 men who embarked only 300 returned in June 1800, the rest having succumbed to the pestilent climate. After a six-month stay in England the regiment was quartered in the Channel Islands, where they remained until the beginning of 1804.

52nd Regiment

In December 1755, under a Letter of Service, Colonel Hedworth Lambton raised a new regiment, the 54th of Foot, the original title of the 43rd Regiment of Foot. In 1757, after various disbandments it was renumbered the 52nd Regiment.

Quartered in England and Ireland, it was not until 1765 that the 52nd had their first taste of foreign service—when it arrived in Canada. During the American War of Independence they suffered heavy casualties, notably at the battle of Bunker Hill, where only eight men of the Grenadier Company remained unhurt. By the autumn of 1778 the regiment had become so weak in numbers that those remaining embarked for England, where they spent the next four years.

The year 1782 saw the introduction of County titles for regiments not already having a special designation, such as 'The King's Own' or 'The Queen's'. The 52nd were styled the 'Oxfordshire' Regiment of Foot.

The 52nd's next tour of foreign service took them for the first time to India, in the Madras Presidency. Soon after its arrival a detachment of the regiment took part in the siege of Cannanore where, 'The resolute and determined efforts of the British Division . . . was worthy of any troops sent abroad by our warlike nation . . .' Here an old soldier named Taylor, who had served in the regiment's Light Company in

Henry Bouquet, appointed in 1756 as first commanding Officer of the 1st Battalion, 60th Royal American Regiment in North America (Royal Green Jackets)

America, received a reward of fifty guineas for some scouting he did under heavy fire. In 1790 the war against Tippoo Sahib started, culminating in the storming of Seringapatam two years later.

In 1800 after a short sojourn in England the regiment, now two battalions strong, took part in the Ferrol expedition and then returned to England in 1801 after having been stationed at Gibraltar and Lisbon.

60th (Royal American) Regiment

In 1755 eleven new regiments of the line were raised, one of them being the 62nd or Royal American Regiment. In 1757, after the disbandment of Colonel Shirley's and Sir William Pepperell's regiments, they were renumbered the 60th. Four battalions were authorised and during the period 1755–83, at least two and often all, were in action in North America against the French and their Indian allies.

In 1763, after the Treaty of Amiens, which confirmed Britain's domination east of the Mississippi, an Indian uprising was led by Pontiac, Chief of the Ottowa tribe. By 1765 all was reasonably quiet again, the Indians having returned to their villages when it became clear to them that the French were not going to help.

In 1797, after the American War of Independence, during which the regiment was in the West Indies, a fifth battalion was raised. This battalion, the first green-coated regular unit in the British Army, was so successful that in 1799 a sixth was raised and despatched to the West Indies to join their comrades. In 1798 the 5th Battalion was engaged in putting down a rebellion in Ireland, and the following year took part in the expedition to Dutch Guiana, where they composed part of the force that captured Surinam. In 1805 the battalion returned home and later went back to Ireland.

95th or Rifle Regiment
Towards the end of the eighteenth century Colonel Coote Manningham and Lieutenant-Colonel William Stewart proposed to the government the raising of a corps of riflemen. The proposal being accepted, a circular, dated 17 January 1800, was issued to the commanding officers of fourteen infantry regiments asking them to '... select from the regiment under your command 2 sergeants, 2 corporals, and 30 private men ...' who were to be instructed as riflemen. In April 1800 the 'Experimental Corps of Riflemen' assembled at Horsham under the command of Colonel Manningham.

At the end of July 1800 a strong detachment of the corps, commanded by Lieutenant-Colonel Stewart, embarked with the Ferrol expedition, with which it did good service in covering the advance of the small British force which attacked on the 25 August. This date on which British Riflemen first came under fire has ever since been observed as the 'Regimental Birthday'.

In 1801 a detachment of the Corps, together with the 49th Regiment (later the 1st Battalion Royal Berkshire Regiment), served with the Fleet under Sir Horatio Nelson at the victory of Copenhagen. These two regiments are the only ones to bear this Naval Battle Honour. It was not until 1951 that both regiments were granted permission to use the Naval Crown superscribed

'2nd. April, 1801' (Army Order 136). Early in 1803 the Corps was renamed the 95th or 'Rifle Regiment'.

The Napoleonic Wars, 1804-1815

In 1803 the 1st battalion of the 52nd Regiment became the 52nd Light Infantry. Its 2nd battalion was separated from it and became the 96th Regiment. In early July, with the threat of a French invasion, the regiment was sent to Shorncliffe, where they were joined in January 1804 by the 43rd, who had also been designated Light Infantry. With the 95th Rifles already at Shorncliffe the nucleus of the famous Light Division was complete. While the troops waited for an invasion that would never come, Sir John Moore, the commander at Shorncliffe, trained his men, sweeping away the time-honoured drill of the eighteenth century and laying the foundation for a new system that would produce 'the thinking fighting man'. It was this perfect training in movement and marksmanship that led William Napier to write of the Light Division, in his *History of the Peninsular War*, 'Those three regiments were avowedly the best that England ever had in arms'.

In 1805, the 43rd and 52nd again raised 2nd battalions, who remained at Hythe and elsewhere in Kent until they were sent on active service in

A silver engraved medal, one-and-a-half inches in diameter, commemorating the 'Victory off Copenhagen' (Royal Green Jackets)

1807 and 1808. A 2nd battalion was also added to the 95th Rifle Regiment, at Canterbury in May 1805 who, in 1807, were employed in the storming of Montevideo and the disastrous attack on Buenos Aires. Later in the same year both battalions of the 95th, along with the 1st/43rd, and the 2nd/52nd, took part in the surrender of Copenhagen under Sir Arthur Wellesley.

In 1803 Britain and France were again at war. At Boulogne Napoleon assembled a large invasion force but soon abandoned the operation and, in 1805, turned his gaze towards Austria, whose army he resoundingly defeated at the battle of Austerlitz. With Vienna and much of his country in the hands of the French, Emperor Francis II was obliged to sue for peace. By 1807 every European port, except those in Portugal, was part of the 'Continental System' and therefore closed to the British. When the Portuguese government rejected Napoleon's command to close its ports, he sent an army under Junot across Spain to occupy the country. The occupation of Portugal inevitably carried with it the occupation of Spain. With the Portuguese Royal Family in exile in Brazil, and Napoleon's brother Joseph supplanting Charles IV as King of Spain, the scene was now more or less set for the start of one of the longest and costliest wars of attrition in the nineteenth century, the Peninsular War.

The year 1808 saw the landing of a British expeditionary force in Portugal under the command of the army's youngest Lieutenant-General, Sir Arthur Wellesley. With this force were four companies of the 2nd/95th and the 5th battalion of the 60th, who were joined into a Light Brigade for the advance on Lisbon. The first shots of the Peninsular campaign were fired by the 95th, who came into contact with the French at the village of Obidos. The enemy evacuated their position but were pursued by the British, who attacked them again near Roliça and drove them off. Wellesley, hearing that reinforcements were about to land at Mondego Bay, halted his force and took up an extended position near Vimiero to cover the disembarkation. With the reinforcements were the 2nd battalions of the 43rd and 52nd regiments.

On the 21st the French attacked the British line but, largely due to the counter-attacks of the

Officer's jacket, 5th battalion, 60th Royal American Regiment c. 1800 (Royal Green Jackets)

43rd and 52nd, they were repulsed. The following is a description of the battle, written by the Adjutant of the 2nd/43rd, Lieutenant Henry Booth:

'About twelve o'clock on Sunday the 21st we saw the French advancing rapidly upon us in large columns to attack our position. They had 14,000 infantry and cavalry, with a large proportion of artillery.

'We had about 10,000, with a small quantity of artillery and only one regiment of cavalry. At half past twelve a heavy cannonading took place on both sides, then they threw several shells with great effect, but our artillery, being remarkably well directed, did considerable execution, in spite of which the French still rapidly and bravely advanced, till both sides came to close quarters. I must observe that our General, being engaged in disposing of the regiments on the right, did not order the 43rd to take a position on the left till the firing from both lines began; of course we were a little too late when we had taken up the position, for the French were literally within five yards of us under cover of an embankment, we were ordered to suspend our fire and retire, to our no small chagrin you may be sure, for had we arrived there a few moments sooner the French could not have forced our position. According to order we retired from a steep hill through a vineyard. The French seeing that gave us a dreadful and well-directed fire which killed and wounded great numbers and threw the regiment in entire confusion for the moment. We rallied a short distance further, and immediately commenced a fire which killed great numbers. The French, being disconcerted, began to retire. We charged them. They were then generally confused, the victory was ours.'

'The Rifles, . . .' according to Rifleman Harris, '. . . as usual were pretty busy in this battle. The French, in great numbers, came steadily down upon us, and we pelted away upon them like a shower of leaden hail. Under any cover we could find we lay, firing one moment, jumping up and running for it the next; and, when we could see before us, we observed the cannonballs making a lane through the enemy's columns as they advanced, huzzaing and shooting like madmen.'

'Such is my remembrance of the commencement of the battle of Vimiero . . . The battle soon became general; the smoke thickened around, and often I was obliged to stop firing and dash it aside from my face and try in vain to get a sight of what was going on, whilst groans and shouts and a noise of cannon and musketry appeared almost to shake the very ground. It seemed hell upon earth.'

A few days later the 1st/52nd landed, but the Convention of Cintra, whereby the French agreed to evacuate Portugal, brought the campaign to an end. The leniency with which the French had been treated caused an uproar in England and resulted in Wellesley and two other generals being recalled for a court of inquiry. The command of the army in Portugal, and the task of clearing the French out of Spain, was given to Sir John Moore who, after concentrating his men around Lisbon, marched north to join up with a force under Sir John Baird who had arrived at Corunna. With Baird were the remaining five companies of the 1st/95th Rifles, four companies of the 2nd battalion, the 1st/43rd regiment and the 2nd/60th.

The 5th battalion of the 60th did not march with Moore's army but remained in Portugal, for its commanding officer had enlisted over a hundred French prisoners into the ranks and Moore could not be certain, when faced by their former friends, where their allegiance would lie.

In the winter of 1808–9 Napoleon himself went to Spain to attempt to set matters right. Seeing the road to France threatened by Moore's advancing army Napoleon turned on him with an enormous force. Due mainly to the abysmal performance of the Spaniards, Moore was forced to retreat towards Corunna in conditions anything but favourable.

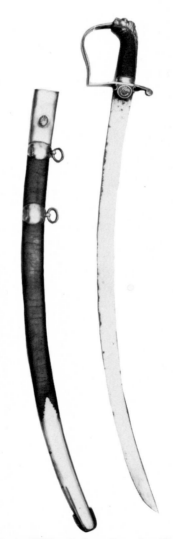

Light Infantry Officer's Sword, c. 1803. This weapon bears on the blade the cypher GR and the regimental number XLIII, denoting the 43rd (Monmouthshire) Light Infantry. (Wilkinson-Latham Collection)

'Winter had now completely set in; ... the weather was unusually severe.' recorded William Surtees of the Rifles, 'Our prospect therefore was by no means a pleasant one. To commence a retreat in front of a greatly superior force, and with the probability that other French armies might be before us and intercept our retreat upon the sea, which was distant from us some 250 miles, with the country in our rear being already exhausted of everything that could contribute to our support, and with such excessively bad weather to perform the retreat in, rendered it, I may say, as unpleasant a situation as troops could well be placed in. Added to which, our commissariat was by no means so efficient ... and our troops in general being young, and unaccustomed to privation, it was but too obvious, that should the retreat continue long, many would be the disasters attending it.'

While the 1st/95th covered the retreat of the main army to Corunna, the 2nd battalion, along with the 1st/43rd and 2nd/52nd, all under the command of Major-General Robert Craufurd, withdrew to Vigo. Even with the appalling conditions, the feared and respected 'Black Bob' Craufurd kept an iron discipline throughout his command. In one instance, when two men were caught straying away from the main body, Craufurd immediately ordered a drumhead court-martial, which duly tried the culprits and sentenced them to receive one hundred lashes each. When the sentence was passed, Craufurd heard a man in the ranks mutter something uncomplimentary and he was ordered immediately three hundred lashes. When darkness fell the column moved on, but stopped at dawn in order that the punishment could be carried out.

Craufurd's footsore and weary men eventually reached their destination, immediately embarked on the waiting transports and after waiting a few

A watercolour by K. M. Clayton depicting the 95th Rifle Brigade at the battle of Waterloo (National Army Museum)

days for stragglers, set sail for Portsmouth.

Meanwhile Moore's army struggled on. Harassed daily by the French they finally reached the heights above Corunna on 11 January. During the next thirty-six hours the bulk of the transport ships arrived and the embarkation began. Just before 2 p.m. on 16 January the French attacked. The battle that followed was a hard fought and costly action, for amongst the casualties was Sir John Moore, who was mortally wounded by grapeshot, his left shoulder shattered and a gaping hole in his left breast with the arm only attached to his body by thin strips of skin. The command passed to Sir John Hope who pressed home the British advance, while Moore was carried back down to Corunna by six soldiers who supported his shattered body in a blanket slung from two poles.

When the French had finally been beaten off the troops embarked on the transports and, leaving their commander buried in the citadel, set sail for England.

On their arrival in England both battalions of the 43rd were quartered at Colchester and those of the 52nd at Deal, where they were rapidly brought up to full strength. The two battalions of the 95th were stationed at Hythe, where they were completed up to a strength of 1,000 men each. So many volunteers came forward that the regiment was granted permission to raise a 3rd battalion. While the 5th battalion of the 60th remained in Portugal, the 2nd battalion was for a short time quartered on the Channel Islands before being despatched to the West Indies.

In April 1809, Sir Arthur Wellesley, restored to his command, arrived in Portugal, spent a week organizing his army and leaving a force to guard the eastern frontier, marched to attack the French Army of the North under Marshal Soult who, with some 13,000 men had reached Oporto. Forcing a passage across the River Douro, Wellesley sent Soult back into Spain and then advanced on Madrid.

After four months at home the 1st/95th Rifles, 1st/43rd and 1st/52nd sailed from England under the command of Brigadier-General Craufurd. On landing in Portugal Craufurd's men marched for Lisbon, then proceeded up the Tagus River in boats and finally began a forced march from Vallada, which Craufurd hoped would bring him into contact with Wellesley whom he knew was in touch with the enemy at Talavera. Unfortunately, by the time the Light Brigade arrived on 29 July, the battle had been fought and the French had withdrawn.

Although the regiments as a whole missed the battle, they were each represented in the action by a single company. In one of his despatches, Wellesley spoke highly of the 5th/60th, whose '... steadiness and discipline ... were conspicuous.' With the British victory at Talavera operations came to a standstill until the following year.

On 26 August 1809, the founder of the 95th Rifle Regiment, Colonel Coote Manningham, died aged forty-four, from an illness brought on by the Peninsular campaign, in which he had commanded a brigade during the retreat to Corunna.

On 22 February 1810, Lord Wellington, as Sir Arthur Wellesley had become, issued a General Order which attached the 1st and 3rd battalions of the Portuguese Caçadores to Brigadier Craufurd's Brigade, which was thereafter to be styled the Light Division. A further General Order, issued on 4 August, divided the Division into two brigades, the 43rd, 3rd Caçadores and four companies of the 95th in one and the 52nd, 1st Caçadores and four companies of the 95th in the other. Also attached to the Light Division was Captain Ross's (Chestnut Troop) of Horse Artillery.

There were four more years of bloody campaigning in the Peninsular in which the Light Division and the 60th participated to the full, earning these regiments numerous battle honours.

BUSACO, 27 September 1810. Wellington, realising that he was too weak to face the immense French army that had poured into Spain retired once again to Portugal. It was at the Ridge of Busaco that he stopped and with his 50,000 men halted Masséna's advance. Five companies of the 60th were engaged and lost five officers and twenty-four other ranks. In his despatch, Wellington specially mentioned the hard work accomplished by the Light Division and recommended that a sergeant from each regiment should be nominated by his commanding officer

'The Morning of Waterloo' by J. D. Aylward. The Duke of Wellington and his staff taking tea with the 95th (Royal Green Jackets)

for promotion to the rank of ensign. As the enemy were too strong to be permanently held Wellington retired to the previously prepared lines of Torres Vedras to winter.

BARROSA, 4 March 1811. In southern Spain part of the 2nd and 3rd battalions of the 95th formed part of the small British division that defeated a French force of nearly twice its strength.

FUENTES D'OÑORO, 3–5 May 1811. In March 1811, Masséna, after a very hard winter, retired to Spain, closely followed by Wellington. At Fuentes D'Oñoro Masséna turned on his pursuers and attacked. At this battle the Light Division and the 60th greatly distinguished themselves.

ALBUHERA, 16 May 1811. A detachment of the Anglo-Portuguese army, which included four companies of the 60th, under the temporary command of William Beresford, beat off a spirited attempt by Soult to break through to the besieged city of Badajoz. It is interesting to note that

Captain John Galiffe and Rifleman Loochstadt, both of the 60th, were present at Fuentes D'Oñoro and Albuhera. Rifleman Loochstadt was one of only two men to receive the Military General Service medal with fifteen clasps. Captain, later Colonel, Galiffe was entitled to fourteen clasps.

CIUDAD RODRIGO, 8–19 January 1812. After ten days of preparation, two breaches were stormed on the evening of 19 January, the lesser breach by the Light Division. The losses on both sides were very heavy, the one most deeply felt by the British was that of 'Black Bob' Craufurd, who was mortally wounded shortly after the assault began.

BADAJOZ, 17 March–6 April 1812. In 1811, Wellington had made an unsuccessful attempt to capture Badajoz in which the British suffered heavy casualties. His second attempt was a success but cost him more than 300 officers and 5,000 men of his Anglo-Portuguese army: the Light Division, under the command of Lieutenant-Colonel Barnard, being amongst the heaviest sufferers. In Wellington's despatch, dated 'Camp before Badajoz, 7 April 1812.' he reported that 'In Lieutenant-Colonel M'Leod, of the 43rd regiment, who was killed in the breach, His Majesty has sustained the loss of an officer who was an ornament to his profession, and was capable of rendering the most important services to his country. I must likewise mention Lieutenant-Colonel Gibbs of the 52nd regiment, who was wounded, and Major O'Hare of the 95th, unfortunately killed in the breach ... Lieutenant-General Picton has reported to me particularly the conduct of Lieutenant-Colonel Williams of the 60th ...'

SALAMANCA, 22 July 1812. The capture of Ciudad Rodrigo and Badajoz opened the road to Spain for Wellington to pursue and engage Marshal Marmont's French army. On 22 July, Wellington pounced on Marmont, inflicting heavy casualties and forcing him to evacuate Madrid. On 31 October, Wellington's army quitted Madrid and began their return march across the Guadarrama Mountains with the Cavalry and Light Division acting as rearguard.

In May 1813 Wellington, with a refreshed and reinforced army, left Portugal and marched northwards, forcing the French to withdraw towards the Pyrénées. Burdened by a large train of waggons and camp followers, King Joseph decided to make a stand at Vittoria. On 21 June Wellington attacked and gained a splendid victory, capturing over 150 guns. The Light Division, divided into two brigades and all the companies of the 5th/60th were heavily engaged.

Accompanying Wellington's despatch was a stand of Colours and the French Marshal Jourdan's baton. In accepting these the Prince Regent wrote to Wellington, on 3 July, 'My Dear Lord,—Your glorious conduct is beyond all human praise, and far above my reward; ... You have sent me ... the staff of a French marshal, and I send you in return that of England.'

Napoleon received the news of the disaster in Spain on 1 July, and realising the consequences it might have, despatched Marshal Soult to command a single unified army in Spain. Unfortunately it was too late, for Wellington pushed the French back across the Pyrénées into France and defeated them at Nivelle, Nive, Orthez and finally laid siege to and stormed Toulouse. On 12 April 1814, news reached Wellington that Russian, Prussian and Austrian troops, Britain's allies, had entered Paris. On 6 April 1814, Emperor Napoleon I abdicated.

Sir William Napier, in his *English Battles and Sieges in the Peninsular*, summed up the six years of bloody conflict when he wrote, '... those veterans had won nineteen pitched battles and innumerable combats; had made or sustained ten sieges and taken four great fortresses; had twice expelled the French from Portugal, once from Spain; had penetrated France, and had killed, wounded or captured two hundred thousand enemies—leaving of their own number forty thousand dead, whose bones whiten the plains and mountains of the Peninsular'.

During the Peninsular War the 5th/60th gained sixteen battle honours and sustained a loss of sixty-eight officers and 767 other ranks killed and wounded, with two officers and 225 men missing. The 1st battalion, which had always been quartered in America, was brought to England, with the 4th battalion, in 1810, but were shortly afterwards sent to the Cape of Good Hope and Dominica. In 1813, two additional battalions, the 7th and 8th, also dressed in green, had been raised at Gibraltar and Lisbon. By 1815, dark green clothing had been adopted by the whole regiment, but as all the battalions were overseas in 1815 they were not present in the Waterloo campaign. After the fall of Napoleon and the return of peace the inevitable reductions in the army followed, cutting the 60th down to two battalions.

The 1st/43rd arrived in England in July 1814 and was quartered at Plymouth where it was soon joined by the 2nd battalion from Hythe. The 1st/52nd, on their return to England, were at Hythe and Chatham. The 2nd battalion, which had gone to Holland in 1813 and Belgium in 1814, later transferred its effectives to the 1st battalion and returned home.

The three battalions of the 95th Rifles arrived in England in July 1814.

On 10 October 1814, the 1st/43rd embarked for America, where it arrived on 31 December in time to take part in the unsuccessful attack on

Ammunition pouch and belt, other ranks, 95th Rifles, c. 1815 (National Army Museum)

New Orleans. Five companies of the 3rd/95th were also present. The operations in North America ended in January 1815, but the 43rd did not arrive in England until June, when they were rapidly made up to full strength and sent to Belgium, missing the battle of Waterloo, but in time for the allied march on Paris.

In January 1815, the 1st/52nd embarked from Portsmouth to Cork, where reinforcements were assembling for North America. Held up by gales they were finally sent to Belgium for Napoleon had escaped from Elba and had landed in France. The Hundred Days had begun.

Within eighteen days of his landing Napoleon was installed in Paris, and Louis XVIII and his entourage had fled to Ghent. Most of the Royalist army and most of its Marshals joined the returned Emperor, who now decided to strike at his two main enemies, Britain and Prussia, massed on his north-eastern frontier.

Within a month of the escape from Elba, Wellington was in Brussels preparing his forces. He was sure that the Corsican would try and destroy his and Blücher's armies separately. But where would the first blow fall?

On 15 June Napoleon crossed the frontier and,

pushing the Prussians before him, got within twenty-five miles of Brussels. At two o'clock on

Officer's belt plate, 1800–1820, of the 52nd Light Infantry (Royal Green Jackets)

12

the 16th, the French attacked on a two-mile front, engaging the Prussians at Ligny and the British at Quatre-Bras. At Ligny they managed to split Blücher's army in two and drive it back to Wavre but at Quatre-Bras their attack was checked. On the 17th, Napoleon sent Marshal Grouchy and 33,000 men in pursuit of the Prussians, while the main weight of his army was flung against Wellington, who had withdrawn his troops to the ridge at Waterloo. On the morning of Sunday 18 June, Napoleon attacked both flanks of the Allied position.

On 22 June, an anxious public was informed, through the columns of *The Times*, that, 'The Duke of Wellington's Dispatch, dated Waterloo, 19 of June, states that on the preceding day BUONAPARTE attacked, with his whole force, the British line, supported by a corps of Prussians: which attack, after a long and sanguinary conflict, terminated in the complete Overthrow of the Enemy's Army, with the loss of ONE HUNDRED and FIFTY PIECES of CANNON and TWO EAGLES. During the night, the Prussians under Marshal BLÜCHER, who joined in the pursuit of the enemy, captured SIXTY GUNS, and a large part of BUONAPARTE'S BAGGAGE. The Allied Armies continued to pursue the enemy. Two French Generals were taken.'

Ensign Leeke, of the 52nd, described his feelings as he faced the enemy on that memorable day. 'I distinctly saw the French artilleryman go through the whole process of sponging out one of the guns and reloading it; I could see that it was pointed at our square, and when it was discharged I caught sight of the ball, which appeared to be in a direct line for me; I thought, shall I move? No! I gathered myself up, and stood firm, with the colour in my right hand. I do not exactly know the rapidity with which cannonballs fly, but I think that two seconds elapsed from the time that I saw this shot leave the gun until it struck the front face of the square. It did not strike the four men in rear of where I was standing, but the four poor fellows on their right'.

In his report to Lord Hill, Sir H. Clinton said that, 'The manner in which . . . the 2nd and 3rd Battalions, 95th under Lieutenant-Colonels Norcott and Ross discharged their duty was witnessed and admired by the whole Army.'

After marching on Paris, the 43rd, 52nd and 95th regiments served with the Army of Occupation before embarking for England.

19th Century Campaigns

43rd (Monmouthshire Light Infantry): 1817, 2nd battalion disbanded; 1824, Gibraltar; 1827, Lisbon; 1831, England; 1835, Canada; 1846, England; 1848, Ireland; 1851, South Africa—2nd Kaffir War; 1852, a draft of one sergeant and forty men, under the command of Lieutenant Giradot, were on board the *Birkenhead* when, seven hours out of Simonstown, she struck a rock and sank off Danger Point; 1853, India.

52nd (Oxfordshire Light Infantry): 1816, 2nd battalion disbanded; 1821, Ireland; 1823, North America; 1833, Ireland; 1836, Gibraltar; 1838, West Indies; 1842, Canada; 1847, England; 1851, Ireland; 1853, India.

60th (Royal American) Regiment: 1824, title changed to 'The 60th Duke of York's Own Rifle

Officer's oval gilt belt plate, with Crown Bugle and number mounted in silver, c. 1810. The wearing of a gilt plate is unusual, as the 43rd (Monmouthshire) Light Infantry were a silver-laced regiment until 1830 (Royal Green Jackets)

Corps'; 1830, title again changed to 'The 60th King's Royal Rifle Corps'; 1845, India—2nd Sikh War, 1849 (1st Btn.); 1851, South Africa—2nd Kaffir War (2nd Btn.); 1855, 3rd battalion re-raised; 1857, 4th battalion re-raised.

95th or Rifle Regiment: 1816, removed from the Line and styled the Rifle Brigade; 1839–46, Ionian Islands, Malta and Canada; 1846, South Africa—1st Kaffir War (1st Btn.); 1850, England; 1851, South Africa—2nd Kaffir War (1st Btn.); 1854, 1st and 2nd battalions proceed to the Crimea

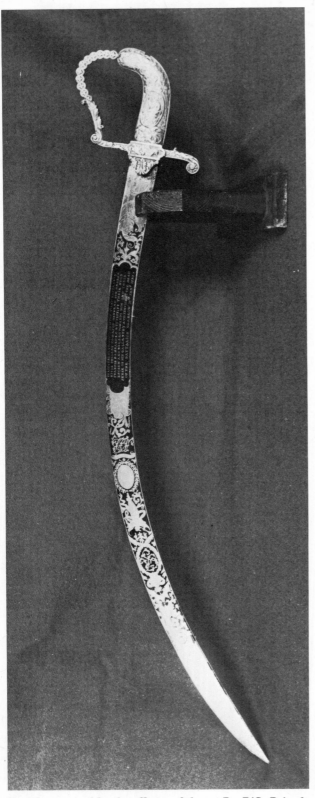

Sword presented by the officers of the 1st Bn. Rifle Brigade to Major General Sir Andrew Francis Barnard, K.C.B. in 1820 (Royal Green Jackets)

where they were engaged at Alma, Inkerman and the siege of Sebastopol. Of the regiment, Major-General Spencer remarked, concerning '. . . their soldier-like qualities and habits of discipline.' that 'The greatest proofs of these are the success which always attended their separate important undertakings against the enemy, and also their speedy recovery from the effects of hardships they, as well as every other regiment in that army, experienced in the winters of 1854–5'; 1855, 3rd battalion re-raised; 1856, 1st and 2nd battalions return to England; 1857, 4th battalion added—2nd and 3rd battalions to India.

In March 1857, the Commander-in-Chief of the Madras Army wrote, 'The loyalty and fidelity of the native troops have been often severely tried . . . But human endurance has a limit and I emphatically warn the Government that the limit has been reached in the army.' Captain Martineau, of the musketry school at Amballa, wrote to a colleague on 5 May, 'I am afraid to say I can detect the near approach of the storm . . . but can't say how, when or where it will break forth . . .' Five days later, on 10 May, 'The Devil's Wind', that was to sweep across Bengal and parts of central India erupted at Meerut, a garrison town some forty miles north-east of Delhi.

The 1st/60th, stationed in India since 1845, formed part of the European garrison at Meerut and were mustering for church parade when the mutiny occurred. The senior officer on parade, Captain Muter, immediately sent a company to secure the treasury and issued ammunition from the regimental magazine. Due to the hesitation on the part of the military commanders, the mutineers were able to leave the town and head for Delhi, the former capital of the Mughal emperor. The next morning, the mutilated bodies of women and children were found everywhere. The 60th, under the command of Lieutenant-Colonel John Jones, '. . . . came upon the corpse of Mrs. Chambers, who had recently arrived from England and was a general favourite in society, lying in a ditch and literally cut to pieces. Horror-stricken at the sight, officers and men raised their weapons in the air and vowed to avenge her death.' The battalion and their leader, known later as 'Jones the Avenger', made good their oath.

Under Brigadier Archdale Wilson the Meerut garrison marched in pursuit of the rebels and fought two actions, in which the battalion took a prominent part. On 7 June, the column joined the army under Sir Henry Barnard at Alighur and moved against Delhi where, after clearing the ridge overlooking the cantonments and the city, they settled in. The siege of Delhi had begun.

The 52nd, at Sealkote when the mutiny began, joined a movable column being formed at Wuzeerabad and for the next three months were at Lahore, Umritsar, Jullundur and other places, taking part in the disarming of various native regiments. In August they joined the force besieging Delhi.

On 13 September, after six days of heavy bombardment, two breaches, one on the right of the Kashmir Gate and the other to the left of the water bastion, were reported practicable, and orders for an assault, to be made by four columns, were immediately issued. No. 1 Column, under Brigadier-General Nicholson, was to storm the breach near the Kashmir Gate, No. 2 Column, under Brigadier William Jones, the breach near the water bastion, No. 3 Column, under Colonel Campbell of the 52nd, which included 200 men of his regiment, were to storm the Kashmir Gate after it had been blown in. No. 4 Column was to capture the suburbs and then enter the Kabul Gate when it was opened by Nicholson. There were also 200 men of the 60th, who were split up in skirmishing order to cover the advance of the assaulting columns.

At daybreak the 52nd had got within 500 yards of the gate. The 60th Rifles covered the advance, with the storming party of the 52nd behind them with, in the rear, the supports and the main body of the column. The bridge in front of the gate had been destroyed but planks were quickly laid across the gap and Lieutenants Home and Salkeld, with a party of Sappers and Miners, went forward to blow the gate open. With the party was Bugler Hawthorn of the 52nd, who was to sound the regimental call as soon as the way was clear. With bullets flying around them, the little group of men managed to lay the charge and set the fuse and with a shattering explosion, the gate was blown in. Lieutenant Home then ordered

Officer, 43rd (Monmouthshire) Light Infantry, c. 1832. (Parker Gallery)

Bugler Hawthorn to sound the advance but, with the noise of the assault, it was not heard. Colonel Campbell witnessed the explosion and ordered his men forward and through the gate.

The assaults were successful and by nightfall the city was partially occupied. It was not until 20 September that the place was completely in British hands.

The siege and capture of Delhi gained two Victoria Crosses for the 52nd—Bugler Hawthorn and Private Smith, and seven for the 60th—Lieutenant Heathcote, Colour-Sergeants Waller

15

and Garvin, Bugler Sutton and Riflemen Divane, Thompson and Turner.

The 52nd were not engaged after the fall of Delhi and spent the winter at Jullundur, returning to Sealkote in 1858 and finally embarking for England in 1864. In 1858 the 1st/60th formed part of the Roorkee Field Force, under Brigadier-General Jones, which operated against the rebels in April and May, then they took part in the campaign in Oudh. The 2nd/60th, which arrived from South Africa in 1858, were engaged in the final suppression of the mutiny.

During the early months of the rebellion, the 43rd were stationed at Madras and Bangalore and it was not until September that they were used for the first time, in disarming the mutinous 8th Native Cavalry at Vellore. Between January and July 1858, the regiment covered 1,300 miles, between Madras and Calpee, clearing the districts of rebels. At the end of 1858, with the mutiny almost completely suppressed, the regiment re-turned to the Madras Presidency until it was ordered to New Zealand in 1863.

On the outbreak of the mutiny, the 2nd and 3rd battalions of the Rifle Brigade were immediately sent from England, landing in Calcutta at different times in November 1857. This was the first occasion that any part of the regiment had served in India. Their first action was at Cawnpore, where the 2nd battalion was joined in the nick of time by the 3rd, who had made a forced march of forty-nine miles in twenty-six hours, dressed in European uniforms and shakos, in intense heat.

It was during the subsequent fighting around Cawnpore that a rather amusing incident occurred. In the course of the 3rd battalion's advance, Captain Atherley's company were nearing the canal when they were approached by an agitated mounted officer who ordered them to fix bayonets. Indignantly, Atherley replied, 'We have not got any bayonets; we have swords.' 'Well,' said the other, 'fix what you have got.' Saying this the officer turned his horse and galloped off.

During the fighting around Lucknow, Captain Henry Wilmot of the 2nd battalion won the Victoria Cross when he kept a large force of mutineers at bay with his revolver, while a wounded man was being removed to safety. Both battalions were mentioned by Major-General Sir James Outram in his despatches; 'The spirit and dash of the men during this critical operation was most remarkable and merits my highest commendation.'

For the remainder of the rebellion, the two battalions were engaged in dispersing and destroying the numerous rebel bands that roamed the countryside. Writing of the 2nd battalion, William Howard Russell, *The Times* correspondent, sent home the following; 'The Rifle Brigade, who are with us, are as hard as nails; faces tanned brown and muscles hardened into whipcord; and to see them step over the ground with their officers marching beside them is a very fine sight for those who have an eye for real first-class soldiers. Lord Clyde is greatly pleased with the officers because they do not ride on ponies as many officers of other regiments are accustomed to do.'

Officer's bell-topped shako, c. 1835 (Royal Green Jackets)

The 2nd battalion remained in India until 1867, when it returned home, but the 3rd did not leave until 1870 and, after spending a year in Aden, arrived at Portsmouth on 1 January 1872.

The 43rd, under the command of Lieutenant-Colonel H. J. P. Booth, reached Auckland (New Zealand) on 11 December 1863, and proceeded to Otahuha. It was not until the end of April of the following year that the regiment encountered the Maoris, when a small detachment, under Major F. M. Colville, was ambushed near Fort Maketu. A week later, in the assault of the Gate Pah, the natives were defeated but only after a very severe combat, in which the 43rd suffered heavy casualties: nine officers, including Lieutenant-Colonel Booth who died of wounds, and thirty-two other ranks. On 21 June Captain F. A. Smith won the Victoria Cross in the action at Tauranga when, although wounded, he jumped down into the rifle-pits and engaged the enemy in a hand-to-hand combat. A number of small actions took place during the next two years after which, in March 1866, the regiment sailed for England. They continued to serve at home, in the Channel Islands and Ireland, until in September 1872, they embarked once again for India. In 1879, the regiment moved to Burma, returning to India in 1882 before embarking for home in January 1887, where they were quartered in the south of England, followed in 1893, by another tour in Ireland.

In March 1865, the 52nd arrived at Portsmouth from India, but the following year they were sent to Dublin, owing to the Fenian riots. The regiment left Ireland in 1868 and after service on Malta and Gibraltar, returned to England in 1874. In 1881, they moved gack to Ireland before moving to Gibraltar, in 1884, and the following year to Egypt, where they supplied a detachment to serve with the Mounted Infantry in the Nile Expedition. During the years 1886–1903, the regiment was stationed at various places in India and took part in the Tirah expedition and numerous other warlike operations on the North–West Frontier.

In 1860, the 1st/60th embarked for England, while the 2nd battalion, under Lieutenant-Colonel F. R. Palmer, set sail for China with the force under General Sir Hope Grant. After taking part in the siege of the Taku Forts and the capture of Peking, the regiment quitted China and by the spring of 1862 were back in England. The 4th/60th were despatched to Canada in 1861, where they helped to guard the frontier while the American Civil War was in progress, returning home in 1869. The year 1867 saw the 1st battalion moved to Canada where, in 1870, they took part in the Red River Expedition against Louis Riel and his followers.

Twenty years after the Mutiny the 2nd/60th were once more stationed in India, taking part in the 1st Afghan War, in which they gained the battle honours, Ahmed Khel, Kandahar and Afghanistan 1878–80. Meanwhile the 3rd battalion was in South Africa, engaged in the second phase of the Zulu War. It was in Zululand that Brevet Lieutenant-Colonel R. H. Buller, later to become one of the most distinguished and controversial military commanders of his day, won the Victoria Cross, when during the retreat at Inhlobane, he rescued Captain D'Arcy and carried him to safety on his own horse. Eighteen months after the Zulu War, the 3rd/60th took part in the disastrous Boer War of 1881.

In 1862, Queen Victoria, '. . . desiring to perpetuate the remembrance of her beloved husband's connection with the Rifle Brigade . . .' commanded that the words 'The Prince Consort's Own' be added to the regimental title. The four battalions of the regiment were very active during the period 1864–98, taking part in many of the small wars and punitive expeditions that occurred during the closing years of the Victorian era:

1st Battalion: Third Burma War, 1885–7.

2nd Battalion: Ashanti War, 1873–4; Nile Expedition, 1884 (detachment); Second Ashanti Expedition, 1895–6 (detachment); Mashonaland Campaign, 1896–7 (detachment); Khartoum and Omdurman, 1898.

3rd Battalion: Nile Expedition, 1884 (Camel Corps); Tochi Expedition, 1897.

4th Battalion: Canada, Fenian Raids, 1865; Expedition against the Jowakis (North–West Frontier), 1877; First Afghan War, 1878–80; Expedition against the Waziris (North–West Frontier), 1881; Pokan Expedition (Burma), 1888–9; Mashonaland Campaign (detachment), 1896–7.

Officers, N.C.O.'s and other ranks of the Rifle Brigade in various orders of Dress, c. 1840. A watercolour by R. Simkin (National Army Museum)

In 1878 a committee was set up under Edward Cardwell to study the organisation of the British Army. In 1881, the findings of the committee were put into effect, converting 109 numbered regiments of foot into territorially-titled regiments. The 43rd (Monmouthshire Light Infantry) and the 52nd (Oxfordshire Light Infantry), were united as the 1st and 2nd Battalions of the Oxfordshire Light Infantry. The 60th King's Royal Rifle Corps just dropped their number and the Rifle Brigade's full title did an about face, from The Prince Consort's Own (Rifle Brigade) to The Rifle Brigade (The Prince Consort's Own).

In 1877 the Transvaal Boer Republic, on the verge of bankruptcy and surrounded by warlike Bantus, was annexed by Britain. Four years later the Boers, under Paul Kruger, regained their independence, after the first Boer War; but in 1886, gold was discovered on the Witwatersrand bringing with it an influx of *uitlanders*. With the arrival of these newcomers fresh tensions developed which culminated in the famous and disastrous Jameson Raid in 1896. In the autumn

of 1899, the long-standing disputes between Britain and the Transvaal came to a head, when Kruger issued an ultimatum to the British Government demanding the immediate withdrawal of her armed forces from the Transvaal's frontier. On Wednesday 11 October, '. . . at tea time . . .', as *The Times* humorously put it, Great Britain and the Transvaal Republic, allied with the Orange Free State, were at war.

The Boer War

The Second Boer War, or South African War, was to prove the greatest conflict in which Britain had been engaged in the nineteenth century since the Napoleonic Wars. This 'Last of the Gentlemen's Wars', which as usual the British public felt sure was going to be a rapid one, lasted two-and-a-half years, cost £222,000,000 and involved 450,000 Imperial troops of which 22,000 died, just under three quarters of them from disease.

After waiting for more than a week on their

A young officer of the 43rd, showing the uniform c. 1850 (Parker Gallery)

the 1st and 2nd battalions were with the 8th Brigade, 5th Dvision until, on 1 August 1900, the 2nd proceeded to Ceylon with a boat-load of Boer prisoners.

The 3rd/60th left England in November 1899, and took part in all the battles for the relief of Ladysmith, including Colenso, where Lieutenant F. H. S. Roberts was killed while trying to save the guns. For this gallant action, he was awarded the Victoria Cross, the first time that the son of a V.C. (Lord Roberts) was similarly decorated.

In August 1900, the 1st/60th were present at the battle at Belfast and subsequently assisted in the occupation of Lydenburg. On 16 October, they returned to Middelburg, where they were continually engaged in many minor operations until July 1901, when they proceeded to the Cape Colony, occupying seventy miles of Blockhouses between De Aar and the Orange River until the end of the war.

The 1st Battalion Oxfordshire Light Infantry (43rd) arrived in Cape Town from England on 14 January 1900, and moved via Naauwpoort, Thebus and Modder River to take part in the operations for the relief of Kimberley. On the morning of 15 February the regiment, after a march of twenty-seven miles, reached Klip Drift and the next day bore the brunt of the fighting at Klip Kraal, sustaining some fifty casualties. Under cover of darkness the Boers, under Cronje, evacuated their position. On the night of the 17/18 February, the battalion, part of the 13th Infantry Brigade, 6th Division, bivouacked some two miles from Paardeberg Drift.

On the morning of the 18th, the British attacked. Severe fighting continued until dark and a very gallant charge cost the regiment in killed and wounded three officers and thirty-two other ranks. Although after twelve hours of continuous fighting the Boer laager remained uncaptured, Cronje's force was now surrounded. During the following week Cronje's position was subjected to a severe bombardment, while the infantry entrenched themselves and waited. At 6 a.m. on 27 February Cronje unconditionally surrendered with 4,000 men. The British now began preparation for the invasion of the Orange Free State.

By 14 March the 6th Division had occupied Bloemfontein, where they remained while Lord

frontiers the Transvaal and Orange Free State burghers advanced. In view of the vast area involved, the Boers moved east and west to cut the railways which were vital to the British. On the west a large portion of track was captured and the towns of Kimberley and Mafeking surrounded.

At Talana Hill, the first clash of the war, the 1st/60th greatly distinguished themselves in the attack on the Boer position. Lieutenant-Colonel Gunning, commanding the battalion, was killed leading his men. Out of seventeen officers, the 1st had five killed and eight wounded along with many N.C.O.s and Riflemen. After the battle a general retirement to Ladysmith was ordered. Joubert's men captured the railway to the south and cut the town off. With the three now famous sieges of Mafeking, Kimberley and Ladysmith under way, thousands of British troops were rendered completely useless.

The 2nd/60th, who had landed in Natal, were in Ladysmith waiting to greet the 1st battalion. After the relief of the town, in February 1900,

Roberts marched on Pretoria, the capital of the Transvaal. During August and September, the regiment was employed in operations against De Wet, marching more than 500 miles before reaching Heilbron on 3 October, where they stayed until June 1901, afterwards moving on to Kroonstad, Bloemfontein and then to Modder River. In September the regiment began block-house duties which occupied it up to the end of the war.

The 2nd Rifle Brigade arrived at Durban, from Crete, and was moved north to Ladysmith, where, only four days after landing, they were besieged in the town. The 1st battalion arrived from Southampton on 25 November and joined Sir Redvers Buller's army. At Colenso the battalion was only lightly engaged but Captain Walter Congreve, serving on the Staff, was awarded the Victoria Cross for trying to save the guns and then, although wounded, returning to rescue Lieutenant Roberts of the 60th.

Five days before the battle of Colenso, on 10 December 1899, five companies of the 2nd/Rifle Brigade carried out a sortie from Ladysmith to destroy a Boer howitzer on a strongly-held height called Surprise Hill. Sergeant W. E. Danton described the way the riflemen fought their way back after having accomplished their mission. 'There was not time for thought but to act at once and fight our way through at the point of the sword; bullets were flying like hailstorms . . . My captain was shot . . . He shouted for me to form up my men and get the wounded inside, which we did; during that time men were shot

Pioneers of the 43rd (Monmouthshire) Light Infantry in Ireland, c. 1850. Note the aprons and various tools worn (Parker Gallery)

20

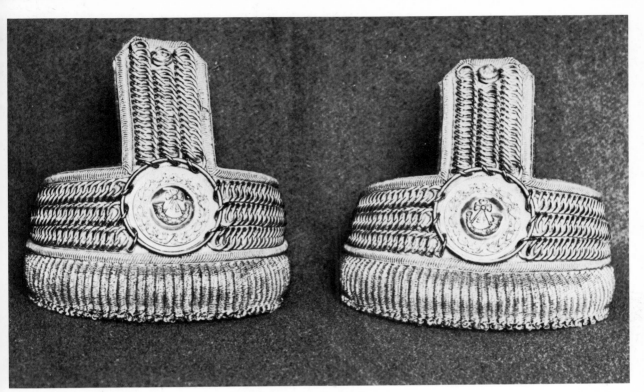

Wing epaulettes of an officer of the 43rd, c. 1850 (Royal Green Jackets)

on each side of me. After forming up we charged the Boers and cut our way through . . . After this we made for our entrenchments at which, thank God, we arrived safely after five hours hard fighting.'

At Vaal Krantz, the 1st battalion, together with the 1st Durham Light Infantry, took a very active part in holding the position they had won for twenty-four hours. One of the correspondents of the *Standard* speaking of this action commented, 'It is to the gallantry of the Durhams and the Rifle Brigade that the achievement of storming Vaal Krantz and the walled farm-houses on the right is due.'

After the relief of Ladysmith, the 2nd battalion was employed in the Eastern Transvaal, on trek in various flying columns and in garrisoning Lydenberg.

In addition to the 1st Oxfordshire Light Infantry, K.R.R.C. and the Rifle Brigade, a large number of men from these battalions were also employed as Mounted Infantry and did some very valuable work. Besides these there was also a composite Rifle Battalion which was formed in Natal from drafts of the 1st and 2nd Rifle Brigade

and the K.R.R.C. Referring to this battalion Sir Redvers Buller said, in his despatch of 30 March 1900, 'I was much struck by the way in which a Battalion made up of drafts . . . and officered by 2nd Lieutenants worked.'

At the conclusion of the war and for the next twelve years, the 1st Oxfordshire Light Infantry, King's Royal Rifle Corps and Rifle Brigade continued to provide garrisons for the Empire— Malta, Gibraltar, India, Burma and Egypt being just a few of the stations at which they were quartered. In 1908, with the disbandment of the 3rd battalion of the Oxfordshire Light Infantry (Royal Bucks Militia), the title of the regular regiment was changed to 'The Oxfordshire and Buckinghamshire Light Infantry'.

As a result of the South African War, a lot of the cobwebs were dusted out of Horse Guards. The tactical errors, bad supply and training forced a wave of reforms which transformed the army into the most efficient regular military force in the world, for its size, and prepared it for the coming conflict which was to shake the foundations of the world.

The Great War

'You are leaving home to fight for the safety and honour of my Empire.

Belgium, whose country we are pledged to   defend,
has been attacked and France is about to be invaded by the same powerful foe.

I have implicit confidence in you my soldiers. Duty is your watchword, and I know your duty will be nobly done.

I shall follow your every movement with deepest interest and mark with eager satisfaction your daily progress, indeed your welfare will never be absent from my thoughts.

I pray God to bless you and guard you and bring you back victorious.'

(His Majesty King George V's message to his troops.)

The Oxfordshire and Buckinghamshire Light Infantry (43rd/52nd)

Battalions raised: seventeen.   Died: 5,878. Battle Honours: fifty-nine, of which the following were authorised to be carried on the Colours and appointments: Mons; Ypres, 1914, '17; Langemarck, 1914, '17; Nonne Bosschen; Somme, 1916, '18; Cambrai, 1917, '18; Piave; Doiran, 1917, '18; Ctesiphon; Defence of Kut al Amara.

The above honours were emblazoned on the King's Colour, and not the Regimental Colour.

Victoria Crosses awarded to the Regiment during the First World War:

Company Sergeant-Major Edward Brooks, 2nd/4th Btn. France, 28 April 1917

'For most conspicuous gallantry. This Warrant Officer, while taking part in a raid on the enemy's trenches, saw that the front wave was checked by an enemy machine-gun at close quarters. On his own initiative, and regardless of personal danger, he rushed forward from the second wave with the object of capturing the gun, killing one of the gunners with his revolver, and bayonetting an-

Sergeant-Major's coatee, 43rd Light Infantry, c. 1850. Note the badge of rank, a crown above four downward pointing chevrons in silver lace, and the use of lace on cuff, collar and wings (Royal Green Jackets)

other. The remainder of the gun's crew then made off, leaving the gun in his possession. Company Sergeant-Major Brooks then turned the machine-gun on to the retreating enemy, after which he carried it back into our lines. By his courage and initiative he undoubtedly prevented many casualties, and greatly added to the success of the operations.'

'During a local operation on the morning of 12 September 1918, in front of Laventie, the flank platoon of A Company, 2/4th Battalion Oxford and Bucks Light Infantry, was held up by heavy and persistant machine-gun fire from a trench about seventy yards distant. Finding it impossible to advance, Lance-Corporal Wilcox crawled towards the trench with four men, bombed it, and finally rushed the nearest to him, disposed of the gunner, and, being unable to take the gun along with him, put it out of action.

'He then worked his way up the trench, bombed the next gun position (during which action two of his section were wounded), and himself again rushed the gun, killed the gunner in a hand-to-hand struggle, and put the gun out of action.

'In spite of the reduced number of his party, this N.C.O. continued his advance up the trench. Bombing the gun positions, he killed one gunner, wounded another, and put two more guns out of action (it still being impossible to dispose of them otherwise), and successfully reached his objective.

'Having by this time only one man with him, Lance-Corporal Wilcox was obliged to withdraw when the Germans counter-attacked in strength. Besides being so extremely outnumbered, he was without fire-weapons, rifles being clogged up with mud, owing to the bad weather before and during the operations. In spite of the very superior numbers against him, he withdrew successfully.'

The King's Royal Rifle Corps (60th)

Battalions raised: twenty-six. Died: 12,842. Battle Honours: sixty, of which the following were authorised to be carried on Regimental appointments; Mons; Marne, 1914; Ypres, 1914, '15, '17, '18; Somme, 1916, '18; Arras, 1917, '18; Messines, 1917, '18; Epehy; Canal du Nord; Selle; Sambre.

Victoria Crosses awarded to the Regiment during the First World War:

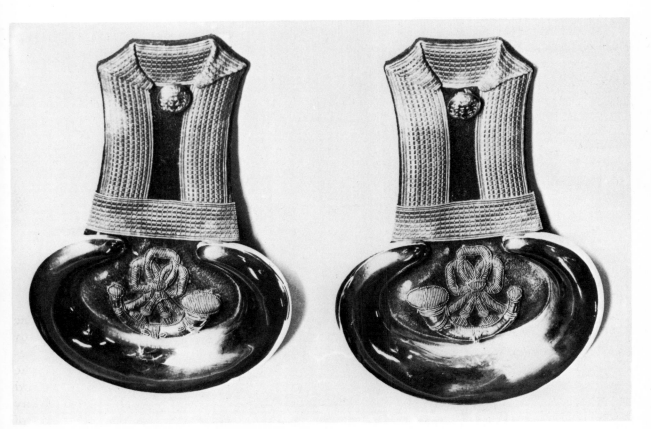

Officers frock coat epaulettes of the 52nd (Oxfordshire) Light Infantry, c. 1852 (Royal Green Jackets)

Rifleman, 60th Rifles, photographed by James Robertson, c. 1855. This photograph shows the uniform and equipment worn during the latter part of the Crimean War (National Army Museum)

1 **Private, Colonel Fowkes' Regiment, 1742**
2 **Grenadier, 43rd Regiment, 1751**
3 **Grenadier, 52nd Regiment, 1768**

2

1

3

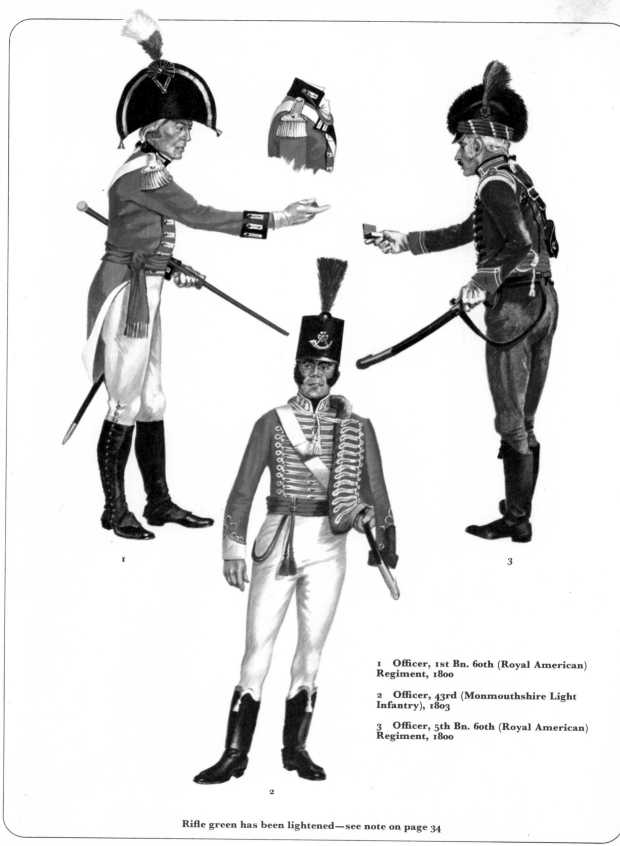

1 Officer, 1st Bn. 60th (Royal American) Regiment, 1800

2 Officer, 43rd (Monmouthshire Light Infantry), 1803

3 Officer, 5th Bn. 60th (Royal American) Regiment, 1800

Rifle green has been lightened—see note on page 34

B

1 Sergeant, 95th or Rifle Regiment, 1809

2 Private, 43rd (Monmouthshire Light Infantry), 1810

3 Officer, 5th Bn. 60th (Royal American) Regiment, 1812

1 **Sergeant-Major, 60th Duke of York's Own Rifle Corps, 1824**

2 **Officer, Undress, 52nd (Oxfordshire Light Infantry), 1835**

3 **Officer, Court Dress, The Rifle Brigade, 1825**

Rifle green has been lightened—see note on page 34

1   Officer, 43rd (Monmouthshire Light Infantry), 1850

2   Private, The Rifle Brigade, 1854

3   Private, 52nd (Oxfordshire Light Infantry), 1857

MICHAEL ROFFE

E

1 **Officer, 1st Bn. The Prince Consort's Own (Rifle Brigade), 1870**

2 **Officer, 52nd (Oxfordshire Light Infantry), 1860**

3 **Officer, 1st Bn. Oxfordshire Light Infantry, 1894**

Rifle green has been lightened—see note on page 34

MICHAEL ROFFE

1   Officer, The King's Royal Rifle Corps, 1898

2   Sergeant, 1st/4th Bn. The Oxfordshire and Buckinghamshire Light Infantry, 48th Division, 1916

3   Officer, Mess Dress, The Rifle Brigade (Prince Consort's Own), 1934

1   Private, 2nd Bn. Oxfordshire and Buckinghamshire Light Infantry, 6th Airborne Division, 1944

2   Officer, 1st Bn. The King's Royal Rifle Corps, 7th Armoured Division, 1942

3   Officer, No. 1 Dress, The Royal Green Jackets, 1970

Rifle green has been lightened—see note on page 34

MICHAEL ROFFE

Lieutenant J. H. S. Dimmer, 2nd Btn., Belgium, 12 November 1914.

'This officer served his machine gun during the attack on the 12 November 1914, at Klein Zillebeke, Belgium, until he had been shot five times—three times by shrapnel and twice by bullets—and continued at his post until his gun was destroyed.'

Captain J. H. P. Butler, K.R.R.C., attached to the Pioneer Company, Gold Coast Regiment, West African Frontier Force. Cameroons, 17 November 1914 and 27 December 1914.

'For most conspicuous bravery in the Cameroons, West Africa. On the 17 November 1914, with a party of thirteen men, he went into the thick bush and at once attacked the enemy, in strength about one hundred, including several Europeans, defeated them, and captured their machine gun and many loads of ammunition. On 27 December 1914, when on patrol duty with a few men, he swam the Ekam River, which was held by the enemy, alone and in the face of a brisk fire completed his reconnaissance on the farther bank, and returned in safety. Two of his men were wounded while he was actually in the water.'

Rifleman W. Mariner, 2nd Btn., France, 22 May 1915.

'During a violent thunderstorm on the night of 22 May 1915, he left his trench near Cambrin, crept through the German wire entanglements and, single-handed, destroyed a German machine gun emplacement that was damaging the British parapets and hindering the working parties.'

Rifleman G. Peachment, 2nd Btn., France, 25 September 1915 (Posthumous Award).

'For most conspicuous bravery near Hulluch on 25 September 1915. During very heavy fighting when our front line was compelled to retire in order to reorganise, Private Peachment, seeing his Company Commander, Captain Dubs, lying wounded, crawled to assist him. The enemy's fire was intense, but though there was a shell-hole quite close, in which a few men had taken cover, Private Peachment never thought of saving himself. He knelt in the open by his officer and tried to help him, but while doing this he was first wounded by a bomb and a minute later mortally wounded by a rifle bullet. He was one of the youngest men in his battalion, and gave this splendid example of courage and self-sacrifice.'

Sergeant A. Gill, 1st Btn., France, 27 July 1916 (Posthumous Award).

'For most conspicuous bravery. At Delville Wood, after a strong German counter-attack, Sergeant Gill rallied the remnants of his platoon, reorganised his defences and managed to hold up their advance. Sergeant Gill was killed when he stood up to direct the fire of his men.

Sergeant E. Cooper, 12th Btn., Belgium, 16 October 1917.

'For most conspicuous bravery and initiative in attack on 16 August 1917, at Langemarck, Flanders. Enemy machine guns from a concrete blockhouse, 250 yards away, were holding up the advance of the battalion on his left, and were also causing heavy casualties to his own battalion. Sergeant Cooper, with four men, immediately rushed the blockhouse though were heavily fired on. About 100 yards distant he ordered his men to lie down and fire at the blockhouse. Finding this did not silence the machine guns he immediately rushed forward straight at them and fired his revolver into an opening in the blockhouse. The machine guns ceased firing and the garrison surrendered. Seven machine guns and forty-five prisoners were captured in this blockhouse.'

Lieutenant-Colonel A. D. Borton, K.R.R.C., Commanding the 2nd/22nd Btn., London Regiment, T.A., Palestine, 7 November 1917.

'For most conspicuous bravery and leadership on 7 November 1917, at Sheria, Palestine. Under most difficult conditions in darkness and in an unknown country, he deployed his battalion for attack, and at dawn led his attacking companies against a strongly held position. When the leading waves were checked by a withering machine gun fire, Lieutenant-Colonel Borton showed an utter contempt of danger, and moved freely up and down his lines under heavy fire. Reorganising his command, he led his men forward and captured the position. At a later stage of the fight he led a party of volunteers against a battery of field guns in action at point-blank range, capturing the guns and the detachments. His fearless leadership was an inspiring example to the whole brigade.'

Rifleman A. E. Shepherd, 12th Btn., France, 20 November 1917.

'For most conspicuous bravery as a company runner on 20 November 1917, at Cambrai. When his company was held up by a machine gun at point-blank range he volunteered to rush the gun and, though ordered not to, rushed forward and threw a Mills bomb, killing two gunners and capturing the gun. The company, on continuing its advance, came under heavy enfilade machine gun fire.

'When the last officer and the last non-commissioned officer had become casualties he took command of the company, ordered the men to lie down, and himself went back some seventy yards under severe fire to obtain the help of a tank.

'He then returned to his company and finally led them to their objective.

'He showed throughout conspicuous determination and resource.'

Rifle Brigade (The Prince Consort's Own)

Battalions raised: twenty-one. Died: 11,575. Battle Honours: fifty-two, of which the following were authorised to be carried on Regimental appointments; Le Cateau; Neuve Chapelle; Ypres, 1915, '17; Somme, 1916, '18; Arras, 1917, '18; Messines, 1917; Cambrai, 1917, '18; Hindenburg Line; France and Flanders, 1914–18; Macedonia, 1915–18.

Victoria Crosses awarded to the Regiment during the First World War:

Company Sergeant-Major H. Daniels and Acting Corporal C. R. Noble, 2nd Btn., France, 12 March 1915.

'On 12 March 1915, Corporal Noble, accompanied by Company Sergeant-Major Daniels, moved forward from their position to cut a way through the barbed wire entanglements which held up the advance of the battalion. Both men were severely wounded but managed to carry out their task, enabling the German trench to be captured. Corporal Noble died of his wounds and was awarded a posthumous V.C. Company Sergeant-Major Daniels recovered from his wounds, was awarded the V.C. and granted a commission. Later he was awarded the Military Cross for an act of bravery at Fromelles in 1916.

2nd Lieutenant S. C. Woodroffe, 8th Btn., Belgium, 30 July 1915 (Posthumous Award).

On 30 July 1915, the Germans launched a sudden attack on the trenches on the outskirts of Hooge. Using the new liquid fire they managed to force the British to retire. Lieutenant Woodroffe's position was attacked from the flank and the rear, but he managed to hold on until his bomb supply was completely exhausted and then withdrew his men in good order. Almost immediately afterwards he led a counter-attack with great bravery, but was killed while attempting to cut a way through the enemy's barbed wire under heavy rifle and machine gun fire.

Corporal A. G. Drake, 8th Btn., France, 23 November 1915 (Posthumous Award).

Returning from a patrol in No Man's Land, Corporal Drake insisted on remaining with a wounded officer, and bandaging his wounds. When a rescue party found them, Drakes body was riddled with bullets.

Major W. La Touche Congreve, 3rd Btn., France, 6–20 July 1916 (Posthumous Award).

'For most conspicuous bravery during a period of fourteen days preceding his death in action.

'This officer constantly performed acts of gallantry and showed the greatest devotion to duty and by his personal example inspired all those around him with confidence at critical periods of the operations. During the preliminary preparations for the attack, he carried out personal reconnaissances of the enemy's lines, taking out parties of officers and N.C.O.s for 100 yards in front of our lines in order to acquaint them with the ground. All these preparations were made under fire. Later, by night, Major Congreve conducted a Battalion to its position of deployment, afterwards returning to it to ascertain the situation after assault. He established himself in an exposed forward position from whence he

Officers of the 3rd Bn. King's Royal Rifle Corps, photographed in Dublin in 1855, in various orders of Dress (Royal Green Jackets)

A group of officers of the 60th photographed inside the Palace at Delhi just after its capture. 'Jones the Avenger', with white beard, is seated in the centre (Royal Green Jackets)

successfully observed the enemy and gave orders necessary to drive them from their position.

'Two days later, when Brigade Headquarters was heavily shelled, and many casualties resulted, he went out and assisted the M.O. to remove the wounded to places of safety, although he was himself suffering severely from gas and other shell effects. He again on a subsequent occasion showed supreme courage in tending wounded under heavy shell fire. He finally returned to the front line to ascertain the situation after an unsuccessful attack, and whilst in the act of writing his report was shot and killed instantly.'

Prior to the award of the Victoria Cross, Major Congreve already held the Distinguished Service Order, Military Cross and Legion of Honour. The award of the V.C. made him the first officer in the Army to hold all four decorations for gallantry. Major La Touche Congreve was the son of Lieutenant-General Sir W. Congreve who won the Victoria Cross at Colenso when a Captain in the Rifle Brigade, a distinction held by only two other families whose father and son had served in the British Army.

2nd Lieutenant G. E. Cates, 2nd Btn., France, 8 March 1917 (Posthumous Award).
'For most conspicuous gallantry and self-sacrifice. When employed with some other men in deepening a captured trench, this officer struck with his spade a buried bomb, which immediately started to burn. 2nd Lieutenant Cates in order to save the lives of his comrades placed his foot on the bomb which immediately exploded. He showed the most conspicuous gallantry and devotion to duty in performing the act which cost him his life but saved the lives of others.'

Sergeant W. F. Burman, 16th Btn., Belgium, 20 September 1917.
For gallantry during the Ypres offensive.

Sergeant W. Gregg and Rifleman W. Beesley, 13th Btn., France, 8 May 1918.
'For gallantry during an attack at Bucquoy led by Sergeant Gregg after all the officers in his company had become casualties. Sergeant Gregg had already been awarded the Military Medal in 1914 and the Distinguished Conduct Medal in 1917.'

Sir Alfred Hastings Horsford, K.C.B., Rifle Brigade, c. 1860. He commanded the 1st Battalion at the Alma, Balaklava, Inkerman and Sebastopol. Colonel-Commandant of the Rifle Brigade from 1880 until his death in 1885. He is wearing the 1855 pattern shako and the tunic introduced in the same year (Wilkinson-Latham Collection)

'Billy the Bugler'. Bandmaster William Miller, Rifle Brigade, photographed in Canada between 1861–9. He is wearing an ivory-hilted scimitar presented to him on his wedding by the Prince of Wales (Wilkinson-Latham Collection)

The general feeling of the soldier at the front can be summed up by the following extract from a letter of a Rifleman, written home a few days before he was killed in action on 8 May 1918.

'Dear Mother, just a few lines to you hoping this letter will find you in the best of health as it leaves me at present. I am getting on allright now. It was a bit strainge the first two or three days but I am getting a bit used to it now but bleeding wars that wants some getting used to I might tell you.'

Between the Wars

The Oxfordshire and Buckinghamshire Light Infantry

1st Battalion

On 4 March 1919, the cadre of the 43rd sailed home from Mesopotamia, arriving on 12 March. After being brought up to strength it formed part of the North Russian Relief Force and sailed for Archangel in May. On 25 June it was in action against the Bolsheviks on the River Vaga, in the attack on Ignatofskaya. In September, after further brushes with Red forces, they withdrew to the base and returned home in October. After a short spell in England they were sent to Ireland in connection with the 'Troubles'.

2nd Battalion

After serving in Ireland the 52nd sailed for India, where they were stationed at Rawalpindi before moving to Razmak on the North-West Frontier. In 1929, the regiment began a five-year tour of duty in Burma, after which they returned to India and were stationed at Mhow at the outbreak of the Second World War.

The King's Royal Rifle Corps

After serving with the Army of Occupation, the 1st and 2nd Battalions returned to England in 1919. In 1920 and '21, both battalions were stationed in Ireland, but at the end of 1922, the 1st sailed for India where they were to take over the duties of the 3rd and 4th battalions who, on returning to England, were disbanded at Winchester in January and February 1923. India remained the home of the 1st battalion until

1934, when, after a spell in Waziristan, they proceeded to Burma and finally in 1938 to Egypt.

In April 1922, the 2nd battalion went to Silesia, then to Cologne, finally returning home in June 1925. In 1936, the battalion was sent to Palestine where they helped quell the Arab revolt, remaining there for fourteen months before returning to England.

In 1937, the 2nd battalion at home was converted to a 'Motor Battalion', as was the 1st battalion a year later.

The Rifle Brigade

In 1921, while the 1st battalion was stationed in India, the 2nd and 3rd were employed in Ireland. The 4th battalion went to India in 1919, but returned home in 1922 where, together with the 3rd, it was disbanded on the general reduction of the Army.

In 1937, the regiment, together with the K.R.R.C., became motorized troops. On the outbreak of the Second World War, the 1st battalion were at Tidworth and the 2nd in Palestine.

Edward, Prince of Wales, in the Rifle Brigade uniform c. 1869 (Wilkinson-Latham Collection)

The Second World War

On Sunday 3 September 1939, at 11.15 a.m., Neville Chamberlain spoke to the nation on the wireless.

'I am speaking to you from the Cabinet Room at 10 Downing Street. This morning, the British Ambassador in Berlin handed the German government a final note, stating that unless we heard from them by 11 o'clock that they were prepared at once to withdraw their troops from Poland, a state of war would exist between us. I have to tell you now that no such undertaking has been received and that consequently this country is at war with Germany.'

The 43rd went to France with the British Expeditionary Force, which fell back fighting on Dunkirk after the collapse of Holland and Belgium and the advance of German troops into French territory.

On 23 May the 30th Infantry Brigade landed at Calais with orders to operate on the enemy's left flank. This Brigade consisted of the 2nd K.R.R.C., 1st Rifle Brigade, 1st Queen Victoria's Rifles and the 3rd Royal Tank Regiment. On the afternoon of the 23rd, the Germans began shelling the town and the next day surrounded it and opened a heavy bombardment. Fighting continued in and around Calais until the 26th when, short of food and ammunition and with numerous casualties, the Brigade was overwhelmed.

On 4 June 1940, the Prime Minister, Winston Churchill, made the following statement in Parliament:

'The Rifle Brigade, the 60th Rifles and the Queen Victoria's Rifles, with a battalion of British tanks and one thousand Frenchmen—in all about four thousand strong—defended Calais to the last.

'The British brigadier was given an hour to surrender. He spurned the offer, and four days of intense street fighting passed before silence reigned over Calais, which marked the end of a memorable resistance.

'Only thirty unwounded survivors were brought off by the Royal Navy, and we do not know the

An officer of the Rifle Brigade in the busby introduced in 1871 (Wilkinson-Latham Collection)

fate of their comrades. Their sacrifice was not, however, in vain. At least two armoured divisions, which otherwise would have been turned against the British Expeditionary Force, had to be sent to overcome them.

'They have added another page to the glories of the Light Division and the time gained enabled the Gravelines Walnlieu to be flooded and to be held by French troops; and thus it was that the port of Dunkirk was kept open.'

The 1st Battalion, King's Royal Rifle Corps

and the 2nd Battalion, Rifle Brigade, formed the motorized infantry units of the 7th Armoured Division's Support Group in the Western Desert. When Italy declared war on 10 June, the Division moved forward to the Libyan frontier and had their first brush with the enemy and captured two frontier posts, Fort Capuzzo and Fort Madalena. In December 1940, General Wavell began his first offensive for Cyrenaica. The operation was a complete success, the Support Group covering the left flank and cutting the enemy's line of retreat to the west at Bardia and Tobruk. In these first operations of the Desert War some 125,000 Italian soldiers were captured, along with tanks, field guns, anti-tank guns and motor vehicles, resulting in the virtual collapse of the Italian Army.

During the three years of desert fighting that was to follow, the two Rifle formations continued to distinguish themselves, Tobruk 1941, Sidi Rezegh 1941, Bir Hacheim, El Alamein and Tunis being just a few of the honours they accumulated while ridding North Africa of Axis troops.

After North Africa came the invasion of Italy with the Allies entering Rome on 4 June 1944. The advance continued, but was slowed up by the withdrawal of troops in preparation for the invasion of France, resulting in the Italian campaign lingering on until April 1945.

After their return from France in 1940, the 43rd was transferred from one formation to another, until it finally became part of the 53rd Welsh Division with which it remained until the end of the war. The 52nd at first formed part of the 31st Independent Brigade, but by 1943 had been moved to the 6th Air Landing Brigade, forming the nucleus of the 6th Airborne Division.

At 11 p.m. on 5 June 1944, a few hours before the main Normandy assault, a *coup de main* party of the 52nd, along with a detachment of Royal Engineers, set off in six gliders for France with the objective of seizing the bridges of Ranville and Benouville over the Canal and River Orne near Caen. Both bridges were taken but not without some difficulty, especially at Benouville Bridge, where the small party were eventually joined by the 7th Parachute regiment and the main body of the 52nd, who reinforced the bridge. In memory of this operation Benouville Bridge

Lucius Falkland Carey, 2nd Rifle Brigade in the uniform worn during the Ashanti War of 1874. Note that officers dispensed with their swords and wore the broad-bladed bayonet designed by Lord Elcho (Wilkinson-Latham Collection)

has since been re-named 'Pegasus Bridge'.

Eleven months after D-Day, on Tuesday 8 May 1945, Winston Churchill made the following announcement from the very same room in which Neville Chamberlain had announced the commencement of hostilities six years previously. 'Yesterday at 2.41 a.m. the representatives of the German High Command . . . signed the act of unconditional surrender of all German land, sea and air forces in Europe . . . The German war is therefore at an end . . . Long live the cause of freedom. God save the King!'

This brief account of the part played by the Green Jacket regiments in the Second World War cannot possibly hope to do justice to the bravery, tenacity and devotion to duty of all ranks.

The following are the Battle Honours won by the three regiments in all the theatres of war.

The Oxfordshire and Buckinghamshire Light Infantry (43rd/52nd) (9 Battalions)

Defence of Escaut; Cassel; Ypres-Comines Canal; Normandy Landing; Pegasus Bridge; Caen; Esquay; Lower Maas; Ourthe; Rhineland; Reichswald; Rhine; Ibbenburen; North-West Europe 1940, '44–5; Enfidaville; North Africa 1943; Salerno; St. Lucia; Salerno Hills; Teano; Monte Camino; Garigliano Crossing; Damiano; Anzio; Coriano; Gemmano Ridge; Italy 1943–5; Arakan Beaches; Tamandu; Burma 1943–5.

The King's Royal Rifle Corps (60th) (11 Battalions)

Calais 1940; Mont Pincon; Falaise; Roer; Rhineland; Cleve; Goch; Hochwald; Rhine; Dreirwalde; Aller; North-West Europe, 1940, '44–5; Egyptian Frontier, 1940; Sidi Barrani; Derna Aerodrome; Tobruk, 1941; Sidi Rezegh, 1941; Gazala; Bir Hacheim; Knightsbridge; Defence of Alamein Line; Ruweisat; Fuka Airfield; Alam el Halfa; El Alamein; Capture of Halfaya Pass; Nofilia; Tebaga Gap; Argoub el Megas; Tunis; North Africa, 1940–3; Sangro; Arezzo; Coriano; Lamone Crossing; Argenta Gap; Italy, 1943–5; Veve; Greece, 1941, '44–5; Crete; Middle East, 1941.

The Rifle Brigade (9 Battalions)

Calais, 1940; Villers Bocage; Odon; Bourguebus Ridge; Mont Pincon; Le Perier Bridge; Falaise; Antwerp; Hechtel; Nederrijn; Lower Maas; Roer; Leese; Aller; North-West Europe, 1940, '44–5; Egyptian Frontier, 1940; Beda Fomm; Mersa el Brega; Agedabia; Derna Aerodrome;

Officers and men of the 3rd Bn. 60th Rifles on the march in Zululand, 1879 (Parker Gallery)

Tobruk, 1941; Sidi Rezegh, 1941; Chor es Sufan; Saunnu; Gazala; Knightsbridge; Defence of Alamein Line; Ruweisat; Alam el Halfa; El Alamein; Tebaga Gap; Medjez el Bab; Kasserine; Thala; Fondouk; Fondouk Pass; El Kourzia; Djebel Kournine; Tunis; Hamman Lif; North Africa, 1940–3; Cardito; Cassino II; Liri Valley; Melfa Crossing; Monte Rotondo; Capture of Perugia; Monte Malbe; Arezzo; Advance to Florence; Gothic Line; Orsara; Tossignano; Argenta Gap; Fossa Cembalina; Italy, 1943–5.

Officer's waist belt clasp, 43rd Light Infantry, c. 1875 (Royal Green Jackets)

* * *

After the war came the inevitable reductions in the Army, phased over a period of years. First came the disbandment of the war-time battalions, followed by the 2nd regular battalions, which were disbanded or were amalgamated with their respective 1st Battalions. In 1958, the Oxfordshire and Buckinghamshire Light Infantry, The King's Royal Rifle Corps and The Rifle Brigade were formed into the three battalions of the Green Jackets Brigade. On 1 January 1966, the Brigade was redesignated The Royal Green Jackets, one of the Army Board's 'Large Regiments'.

Even though the Oxfordshire and Buckinghamshire Light Infantry, The King's Royal Rifle Corps and The Rifle Brigade have now lost their official individuality, their history will always be remembered. The three battalions of the Royal Green Jackets keep alive the identity of their regimental forebears, whose traditions are honoured. The rationalisation which is demanded by modern military conditions need not mean the loss of that regimental morale and character so central to the British Army's traditions, if the will to preserve it survives. In recent years the Light Infantry and Royal Green Jackets have emerged once again as units with a deliberately fostered élite character, and repeated tours of duty under the harsh conditions of Northern Ireland have failed to damage this fine self-confidence.

Officer's helmet plate of the Oxfordshire Light Infantry. This pattern, with change of crown in 1901, was worn from 1881 until 1908 (Royal Green Jackets)

Officers Green Cloth helmet of the 60th, King's Royal Rifle Corps, worn from 1881 until the adoption of the sealskin cap in 1890 (Royal Green Jackets)

The Plates

Since true rifle green is so nearly black, we have followed established convention by lightening the shade in the colour plates so that detail would not be lost.

A1   Private, Colonel Fowkes' Regiment, 1742.
The headdress worn by battalion companies of regiments of the line at this period was the tricorn hat. It was of black felt, with the turned-up brim edged in white tape and had a black bow on the left side. The coat was long, faced in lightish green, and in the case of the 43rd, had no lace. The large white leggings were found unsuitable for marching as they quickly became soiled, so in 1744 Colonels were ordered to provide grey leggings for marching and other duties.

A2   Grenadier, 43rd Regiment, 1751.
The dress of grenadiers at this period is very clearly shown in the Morier paintings in the Royal Collection at Windsor. The cap had the front in the facing colour, embroidered with the Royal cypher surmounted by a crown. The flap on the front was in red material and bore an embroidered White Horse of Hanover and the motto, *Nec Aspera Terrent*. The coat was red with white facings and turnbacks. The regimental pattern lace was of white worsted with red and blue lines and stars, and was sewn on the edge of the lapels, cuffs and waistcoat and as loops across the chest.

A3   Grenadier, 52nd Regiment, 1768.
In 1768, a Royal Warrant was issued abolishing the cloth grenadier cap and replacing it with a black fur one which bore a black japanned plate on the front with the King's crest and motto raised in white metal. The coat was also affected by the warrant. It became shorter, tighter and had lapels that were permanently turned back. The old patterned white gaiters had, by this time, been replaced by black ones.

Maxim Gun detachment, 1st Bn. King's Royal Rifle Corps, Chitral Campaign 1895 (National Army Museum)

Men of the Rifle Brigade pulling a pom-pom gun out of action during the Boer War, 1899–1902 (National Army Museum)

B1   Officer, 1st Bn. 60th (Royal American) Regiment, 1800.

Even after the raising of the 5th Battalion, the 1st continued to wear normal infantry dress: large cocked hat, scarlet coat with blue facings, silver buttons with silver lace button loops and a crimson waist sash. The crossbelt was ornamented with a silver plate engraved with the Garter Belt and motto 'Honi Soit Qui Mal y Pense' surmounted by a crown; in the centre of the Garter Belt was the number 60.

B2   Officer, 43rd (Monmouthshire Light Infantry), 1803.

On the formation of the Light Division by Sir John Moore, the 43rd adopted a scarlet *pelisse* edged with grey fur and laced in silver. This change in dress was probably brought about by a feeling of competition with the 60th and 95th Regiments, who continued to wear clothing very similar to that of the light cavalry. The shako was of black leather with a green plume fitted on the top and a silver bugle badge on the front. The cavalry theme continued through the rest of the uniform with a silver-laced jacket, a barrelled sash at the waist, tight pantaloons and Hessian boots.

B3   Officer, 5th Bn. 60th (Royal American) Regiment, 1800.

In 1797, it was decided to raise a unit in the British Army based on the lines of the German

Jäger battalions—the 5th Battalion of the 60th (Royal American) Regiment.

The officers' full dress was similar in many ways to the light cavalry at this period, having the Tarleton cap for a headdress and a short green jacket, laced across the front in black with three rows of silver buttons. The cavalry influence was carried right through the uniform with the use of a red barrelled sash at the waist, a curved bladed sword, tight green pantaloons and black Hessian boots. The crossbelt, in black patent leather, was ornamented with a lion's head, chains and whistle and a Maltese Cross badge, all in silver, and the cap with a silver-buttoned red cockade, with plumes and with a silver-chained green turban.

C1   Sergeant, 95th or Rifle Regiment, 1809.

This illustration, based on contemporary information and the picture 'The Rear Guard' by J. P. Beadle, depicts the uniform of the regiment on the retreat from Corunna. The coat was dark green with black facings, the collar, cuffs and shoulder straps being edged in white. The sergeant's waist sash had a central line in the facing colour. The 95th were armed with the Baker rifle which had a range of some 300 yards.

C2   Private, 43rd (Monmouthshire Light Infantry), 1810.

The black shako was ornamented with a silver bugle badge and a green worsted tuft on the top

A young officer of the Rifle Brigade c. 1900 (Wilkinson-Latham Collection)

front. The coat was of red cloth with white collar and cuffs, the collar being edged in regimental pattern lace. The buttons on the front were in pairs, each one having a button loop in regimental lace.

C3   Officer, 5th Bn. 60th (Royal American) Regiment, 1812.

By 1802, the Tarleton cap had been discontinued for officers of the 60th and replaced by a shako similar to that worn by the men. The only new piece of clothing adopted around this time was the pelisse, which was of dark green cloth, laced in black and edged in brown fur. The overalls, as shown, were sometimes reinforced with leather inside the legs and around the bottoms.

D1   Sergeant-Major, 60th Duke of York's Own Rifle Corps, 1824.

The broad bell-topped shako, modelled on the contemporary French pattern, was made of black felt and had a leather top. The round shako plate was made of bronzed metal. The most striking features of the shako were the black horse-hair falling plume and the green plaited cords which were fixed to either side at the top and hung down above the peak.

The coatee was of rifle green cloth and had three rows of buttons down the front. The collar and cuffs were faced in scarlet, which in the case of the Sergeant-Major were heavily ornamented with black tracing braid. The rank badge was all in gold lace and embroidery. In the centre of a laurel wreath were four stripes surmounted by a stringed bugle with the number '60' within the strings and the motto *Celer et Audax* below. Above the bugle was a crown.

D2   Officer, undress, 52nd (Oxfordshire Light Infantry), 1835.

The forage cap was in dark green cloth with a black leather peak and chinstrap and a black silk oakleaf pattern lace band with the badge, a stringed bugle and the number '52', above.

The frock coat was dark blue, single-breasted with eight buttons down the front and two small buttons on each cuff. The shoulder straps were of dark blue cloth, edged in gold lace and ornamented with a gilt metal crescent with a gold embroidered bugle.

D3   Colonel-in-Chief, Court Dress, The Rifle Brigade, 1825.

This illustration shows the Court Dress of the Rifle Brigade as worn by the Duke of Wellington when he was Colonel-in-Chief of the regiment (1820–56).

The coatee was of dark green cloth with black velvet collar, cuffs and plastron front. The turnbacks were white. The edge of the collar and cuffs were ornamented with silver embroidery. The epaulettes were in silver lace with a silver metal crescent at the end and a crown and Garter Star, in heraldic colours, on the boards. The pantaloons were of white cloth and were worn with Hessian boots ornamented round the top in black lace with a black tassel on the front.

gilt metal with a silver bugle, within a laurel wreath, with the number '43' in the centre of a circle inscribed 'Monmouthshire'.

E2 Private, The Rifle Brigade, 1854.
The shako was the Albert pattern, with leather top and front and back peaks and a bronze bugle badge on the front. The double-breasted coat was of rifle green cloth, as were the trousers, with black facings. The waist belt and equipment straps were all in black leather.

E3 Private, 52nd (Oxfordshire Light Infantry), 1857.
This illustration shows the typical dress of the 52nd during the siege of Delhi, and is taken from a contemporary description. The headdress was the forage cap, worn with a khaki cover and neck curtain. The flannel shirt was dyed khaki and in some cases was worn outside the trousers. According to the same source the water bottle at this time was 'a common lemonade bottle'.

F1 Officer, 1st Bn. The Prince Consort's Own (Rifle Brigade), 1870.
This illustration, taken from a contemporary photograph in the author's collection, shows the pattern of winter dress worn by the regiment in Canada.

The hat, mittens and great-coat collar were of black Astrakhan fur. The double-breasted coat was of green cloth and had the leading edge decorated with black lace and the front with horizontal bars of black lace across the chest, which were used to close the coat by fastening on to black olivets.

Sergeant's tunic and other ranks' helmet of the Oxfordshire Light Infantry. c. 1900

E1 Officer, 43rd (Monmouthshire Light Infantry), 1850.
The double-breasted coatee was of scarlet cloth with white facings, the collar being ornamented with two buttons and gold lace button loops on each side and the cuffs with a slashed flap with four buttons and gold lace loops. The skirts were white and had a slashed flap with buttons and loops. The Albert pattern shako, introduced in 1844, was made of black beaver with a leather top, and front and back peaks. The plate was in

F2 Officer, 52nd (Oxfordshire Light Infantry), 1860.
The Albert pattern was made obsolete in 1855 by the introduction of a much smaller shako based on the contemporary French pattern. The star plate was in gilt metal with the bugle badge and number within a Garter Belt bearing the motto *Honi Soit Qui Mal y Pense.*

The single-breasted tunic was of scarlet cloth with buff facings, the cuffs and skirts being ornamented with a slashed panel with gilt buttons and gold lace button loops. A crimson net sash was worn over the left shoulder, passing under a crimson shoulder cord, and had tassels hanging on the right side.

F3 Officer, 1st Bn. Oxfordshire Light Infantry, 1894.

The spiked helmet, based on the German *Pickelhaube*, was of green cloth with gilt metal fittings, the star plate on the front bearing the regimental badge within a Garter, the whole being surrounded by a wreath of laurels. On the bottom of the wreath was a silver scroll bearing the title 'The Oxfordshire Lt. Infy.'.

The scarlet tunic had white facings, the collar being edged in gold lace and ornamented with a regimental pattern button and a two-and-a-quarter inch strand of gold Russia braid. The cuffs were pointed and decorated with gold lace and Russia braid. In Levée Dress the swordbelt and slings were of gold lace with a central stripe of crimson silk. The sash, also of gold lace, had two crimson stripes. Trousers were of dark blue cloth with a gold lace stripe down the outside seam of each leg.

G1 Officer, The King's Royal Rifle Corps, 1898.

The black lambskin busby was first introduced for Rifle regiments in 1873, made obsolete in 1878 by the spiked helmet with bronze fittings and finally re-introduced in 1890. The plume was of black eagret feathers with a scarlet vulture feather base. Below the plume was a black corded boss, ornamented with a crown in bronzed metal. Below the boss was the Maltese Cross badge, also in bronze. The black square corded plait was attached to each side of the busby and hung down on the front.

The tunic, of Rifle green cloth, was single breasted and had the front decorated with loops of black square cord with netted caps and drops, fastening with black olivets. The crossbelt and pouch were of black patent leather with silver fittings.

The 2nd Battalion, Oxfordshire and Buckinghamshire Light Infantry charging the Prussian Guard at Nonne Bosschen, November 11th, 1914 (Royal Green Jackets)

The commanding officer and the Band of the 4th Battalion, Rifle Brigade. This photograph was taken in 1922, the year of the battalion's disbandment (Bivouac Books/Jack Blake)

G2 Sergeant, 1st/4th Bn. The Oxfordshire and Buckinghamshire Light Infantry, 48th Division, 1916.

The khaki serge tunic had a stand-and-fall collar and fastened down the front with five General Service buttons; the trousers were of the same material and were normally worn with khaki puttees and black boots. The shoulder straps bore the regimental title in brass. The steel helmet was introduced into service in 1916 to replace the khaki peaked forage cap, and was often covered with hessian in the field. The use of thigh-length rubber waders by troops in flooded or foul trenches is attested by contemporary photographs.

The webbing equipment is the 1908 pattern, and the rifle is the ·303 Short Magazine Lee Enfield.

G3 Officer, Mess Dress, The Rifle Brigade (Prince Consort's Own), 1934.

The Mess jacket was of rifle green cloth with a black silk roll collar and black velvet pointed cuffs. A small silver bugle badge was worn on each lapel. The shoulder cords were of square edged black cord with miniature black metal rank badges. The vest was also in dark green cloth, open in the front, and fastened with four black buttons of regimental pattern.

H1 Private, 2nd Bn. Oxfordshire and Buckingham-shire Light Infantry, 6th Airborne Division, 1944.
In 1941, a rimless steel helmet and the Denison camouflaged smock were general issue to Airborne troops. The helmet had webbing straps and a rubber cup that fitted over the chin. Ordinary battledress trousers with gaiters and black boots were worn. The weapon is the 9 mm. Sten SMG.

Officers White Wolseley Pattern Helmet. Note the silver badge and green pugri. c. 1935

H2 Officer, 1st Bn. The King's Royal Rifle Corps, 7th Armoured Division, 1942.
Regulation dress consisted of khaki drill shirt and shorts (or long trousers), the khaki Service Dress peaked cap with officers' badge (silver bugle on red cockade) and black strap and buttons, and ankle boots or shoes worn with long woollen hose. All ranks and units of 8th Army were notorious for their sartorial individuality, however, and the practicalities of desert warfare led to a most relaxed attitude to dress regulations. The corduroy trousers and rubber-soled suede 'chukka boots' were far more practical than the official dress, and woollen sweaters—sometimes with black-on-red rank badges added to the shoulders, as here—were widely worn. The revolver holster was often worn clipped to the bottom of the ammunition pouch.

H3 Officer, No. 1 Dress, The Royal Green Jackets, 1970.
The modern No. 1 Dress is entirely of Rifle green cloth, cap, tunic and trousers. The cap has a black leather strap across the front, fastening to a small black button at each side. The badge, in silver metal (anodised for other ranks) is the Maltese Cross, bearing the regiment's battle honours, a stringed bugle and the title, surrounded by a laurel wreath surmounted by a crown. The crossbelt is in black plastic or black patent leather with silver metal fittings.